Churches

*A typical rounded Norman doorway,
pillared with carved capitals, Newington
Church, Oxfordshire*

*Twelfth-century font in St Nicholas's
Church, Brighton, Sussex, depicting the
last supper*

Churches
Henry Pluckrose

Mills & Boon
ON
LOCATION
Book no. 1

Photographs and drawings by Alec Davis

MILLS & BOON Limited, London

First published in Great Britain 1973
by Mills & Boon Limited, 17–19
Foley Street, London W1A 1DR.

ISBN 0 263 05297 4 (cased)

ISBN 0 263 05423 3 (limp)

Printed in Great Britain
by W & J Mackay Limited, Chatham
Bound by Hunter & Foulis,
Edinburgh

Contents

Preface

This is not just another book on churches – it is rather a book of clues to help you look more closely at the churches you visit.

Essentially it is written for the young person who wants to know what to look for in an old church and how to record the things he sees.

But I hope it will also be of use to older people who, when touring, drop in and out of churches and find they need a simple visual glossary of architectural terms to give meaning to guide books written by worthy local historians!

February 1972   *H.P.*

The granite church of St Levan, Cornwall

1 Why churches?

There can be few villages or towns in Britain that have not got a church, and it is for this reason that churches have always been of interest to the historian, the social scientist – and the curious. The local church is often the only institution which has survived the passing of time. Some villages, for example, can proudly boast a Norman church. Think for a moment of all the people who might have stood before its altar – a Norman Knight and his lady, a crusader about to join King Richard in the Holy Land, a pedlar returning from a great Mediaeval Fair, the servant of a cavalier fleeing from Cromwell's Ironsides . . . a Victorian chambermaid and her bridegroom, a British airman soon to be engaged in the Battle of Britain and even you, the reader of this book.

If you decide to make a study of churches it hardly matters where you live. Churches are commonplace. Indeed the church around the corner is as good a place as any to begin to learn the art of looking. In fact the local church – because it *is* local and you can visit it time and time again at absolutely no cost – makes the ideal starting place.

But before examining what to look for in a church, it would be as well to understand something of the reasons for it being there at all. Christianity first came to Britain in Roman times. We know, for example, that Alban, a prominent citizen of Verulamium, was executed in 304 for giving help to a Christian priest. Alban became the first British martyr and the city in which he lived is now named after him.

When the Romans left Britain in 410 the country was attacked and finally conquered by the Angles, Saxons and Jutes. But the Christian religion did not disappear entirely. It must have been a great comfort to St Augustine, when he landed in Kent in 597 to convert Britain once more to Christianity, to learn that although King Ethelbert was a heathen, his wife, Queen Bertha, was already a Christian. Augustine's mission is usually regarded as the beginning of the Christian Church in Britain, for even the fierce Viking attacks of the eighth and ninth centuries did not prevent Christianity spreading across the country. Indeed when in 878 King Alfred defeated the Danes at the Battle of Wedmore, he insisted

The Saxon stone church at Bradford-on-Avon, Wiltshire

that Guthrum the Danish leader become a Christian, an example followed by his chieftains and their followers.

Thus churches – places in which Christian priests could perform their religious rites and ceremonies – began to be built. Travel was difficult, the roads were poor and it was necessary for each small community to have its own religious meeting place. The first churches were probably built of wood. Britain was heavily forested, and although stone churches were built in Saxon times, wood was easier to obtain and to work.

But it is with the coming of the Normans under William the Conqueror in 1066 that building in stone really came into its own (though we should remember that even the Normans tended to build in wood

This typical Saxon window is normally only found in towers, but in this church at Worth, Sussex, it lights the nave

when they first arrived; replacing their original wooden castles and churches with stone ones probably took over fifty years). In Norman times stone was quarried wherever it could be found and was transported by boat and cart. If the stone was particularly beautiful and worked easily it was carried considerable distances. Caen stone, for example, was brought from Normandy, while the fine marble of Purbeck (Swanage, Dorset) may be found in churches across the length and breadth of Britain.

Churches were thought of as 'The House of God' and because of this they were made with tremendous care, often being the best building in the village. The priest who worked in the church was expected to be able to read and write. Although some were very poor scholars the priest still had more learning than the ignorant farm labourer, and he became a central figure in the life of the area. He baptised the babies, taught the scriptures, took the marriage services and eventually (or the priest who came after him) buried the parishioners in the churchyard. This is an important thing to understand, for it tells us why our churches are so rich in history. Men are born, marry, die . . . but the church continues because it is never without living members. An old priest may die, but he is replaced by a younger man who continues the practices and customs of the priest who was there before him.

A highly-decorated chantry – the Clopton Chantry Chapel of Long Melford, Suffolk, built about 1496

To our ancestors the church seemed timeless. Because it was concerned with life and death and life after death, it was powerful. Many wealthy people gave property to the church. In return, the church would be expected to provide a decent place of burial and to remember the dead person in prayer. Important local people – mayors, knights and lords –

were buried within the church, the spot being marked with a brass, an incised stone or a plain slab. As time passed the memorials became more and more elaborate, taking up so much space that chapels were attached to the tombs so that prayers could be said for the souls of the departed. Many of these 'chantry chapels' were torn down at the time of the Reformation (Henry VIII, Elizabeth I), the monies for their upkeep being taken by the Crown.

Some churches benefited in even more practical ways. Rich wool merchants, for example, built and extended many of the churches in Eastern England. A well-kept parish church was the sign of a prosperous local community. Craftsmen in wood, stone, silver and gold were employed to make 'God's House' as beautiful as possible. Occasionally artists were commissioned to illustrate religious stories by covering the walls with murals (and this was a good method of teaching at a time when few people could read or write and when books were rare and expensive to produce). This is why some of our smallest villages contain enormous churches. In the Middle Ages the village was probably an important place. As Britain became an industrial country, its importance declined and all that

Long Melford, a fifteenth-century Suffolk 'Wool' church

A mural painting of St George and the
Dragon in Pickering Church, Yorkshire

remains to remind us of its former
glory is the church.

In Elizabethan times the priest was
given an extra task – to record in his
registers all those who were baptised,
married and buried in the church
(remember that it is only quite
recently that non-church marriages
have been possible). This meant that
the church was given the task of
keeping details of people's lives. By
referring to the registers it is possible

to discover something of our ancestors – how long they lived, at what
age they married, the size of their
families as well as the jobs that they
did. This sort of information can be
most useful when engaged in local
studies. If we want evidence of how
some national or local disaster
affected an area, a glance through the
parish registers will often give much
of the information we require. The
registers of All Hallows by the Tower,
London, for example, clearly show

the effect of the plague during the months June to August 1665 on one of the most densely populated parts of the city. I wonder whether the registers of St Mary's, Lambeth (some three miles away) list as many deaths for these months? And the village or town you live in—was it affected at all?

There is always a danger, I suppose, of thinking that churches are only interesting because they are old, full of tombs of knights or mediaeval merchants. Some of the most attractive and fascinating churches I have been in are far from ancient – churches built in Victorian times of brick and slate, or more recently of glass and concrete. What we must do if we are to learn about building styles is to look at every building against the background of its own time. After all, a Norman church was new once and I would not be surprised to discover that the villagers had remarked to one another on the day of the very first service, 'Don't like that there new church. Real ugly I call it.'

In describing the growth of the church as a centre of local life, I have touched upon its purpose – a focal point in the worship of God. This religious aspect – which, after all is the reason for it being there at all – needs to be understood. The builders of our churches tended to work to a pattern. At one end of the church there had to be the altar where the priest could perform the most important of his religious ceremonies. This was usually placed at the eastern end of the church. Some experts suggest that this is because the Holy Land lies to the east of the British Isles. Others think that the reason is quite different. St Augustine realised that one way of encouraging people to become Christians was to put their heathen customs into a Christian setting. The sun, which rose in the east and set in the west, had always played a part in the old religion. To face the rising of the sun to pray was an established custom. Why not build the altars so that the sun rose upon them? Whichever explanation is the true one, the fact remains that most churches in Britain lie along an east-west axis (a useful thing to remember when trying to set an Ordnance Survey map without a compass).

Then, in addition to the altar, there had to be a place for the congregation to stand. The nave or body of the church fulfilled this function. This simple plan was added to – with side chapels and aisles, a place for the choir and a 'crossing place' under the tower or spire. But these are really extras which came later as the community grew richer and as building techniques improved. These are examined in detail in the chapters which follow.

2 Making a record

Before going to visit a church it is wise to decide how you are going to record the things you see. You might prefer, for example, simply to collect postcards, leaflets and guide books or take your own photographs to mount in a scrapbook. But the purpose of a book of this sort is to encourage you to make a collection of your own drawings, rubbings and models (see Chapter 8) and to supplement them with your own notes.

For drawing out of doors it is helpful to have a board on which to rest your paper. A piece of hardboard (approx 18″ × 12″) is ideal, but stout card will do almost as well. One large bulldog clip will be sufficient to hold the paper secure while you are working.

If you particularly enjoy drawing in pencil, experiment by taking a range of grades (I suggest 3H, 2H, HB, B, 2B, 3B). 'H' pencils have a hard lead and give a sharp firm line; 'B' pencils are soft and give a darker gentler line. The 'HB' is the pencil we most often use for writing, and this lies between 'H' and 'B' (i.e. it is neither very hard nor very soft). 'F', which we need not bother about here, is the grade between 'H' and 'HB'. Pencils, though, get blunt quickly and a good quality pencil sharpener is an essential piece of equipment. Buy one that has a container for the sharpenings – these models are so much cleaner when working indoors.

Felt pens (particularly those containing water-based ink) and bamboo and fibre-tipped pens are also excellent for architectural sketches. They are available in a whole range of colours and can be intermixed to produce a variety of subtle tones. The colours can be thinned by dampening the paper with water before it is worked on (a wet finger does very well!). The blurred effect this gives is useful for heightening areas of shadow or to give texture to wood and stone. In this connection I should also mention charcoal which, when used with soft white, red and yellow chalks, is one of the most effective picture-making materials available. The trouble with charcoal, chalks and pastels is that they are messy in use and that drawings need fixing as soon as they are finished. All are excellent for outdoor work, but not for work within the church itself.

Wax crayons are also available in a wide range of colours – including silver and gold. Some (like Finart) are thin enough to be sharpened like a pencil, and it is this type which I suggest you use for your drawings. Crayons give a much stronger line than pencil or felt/bamboo-tipped pens. Because of this you can add an extra dimension to your pictures by working with them on pastel papers (cinnamon, deep reds, greens and blues, stone, daffodil). Wax crayon pictures may also be overworked with water-colour washes. This process, known as a resist, enables us to add colour to any part of the drawing without spoiling the original composition lines. The water-based paint is repelled by the waxed lines, and stains only those areas of paper which have not been crayoned.

Wax crayons can also be used for taking rubbings of churchyard memorials, brasses and commemorative plaques. For this use the thick 'infant' crayon (Freart). Let us assume that you wish to take a rubbing from an old brass which is set in the floor. Dust the brass lightly with a soft cloth, working from the centre towards the edges to remove all particles of grit. Cover the design with a sheet of detail paper and, holding it in position, fix each corner with masking tape, Sellotape, lead weights (or something similar). Feel for the edge of the brass and work the crayon in firm even strokes across the paper. Work from top to bottom of the design, taking care not to scribble or tear the paper. Rubbings may be taken in the same fashion from memorials set in walls. For this, of course, masking tape is essential. Once you have the knack, experiment by rubbing in gold or silver crayon or even in white.

A rubbing in white crayon on white paper might at first seem pointless. But remember that a waxed impression will resist water-based paints and inks. If a rubbing is taken in white it could be resisted with black washable ink or with Brusho or Dylon cold dyes. The effect of the colour will be to throw the white rubbing into striking relief.

Remember before rubbing any brass or memorial inside the church you must obtain permission. The churchyard will probably contain many fascinating memorials upon which to experiment first. Indeed if you really become interested in epitaphs you may find that you rarely go inside a church before reading all the headstones for fear you miss some like these:

**Under this stone
lieth
the broken remains
of
Stephen Jones
who had his leg cut off
without the consent of Wife or
friends on 23rd October 1842
In which day he died
Aged 31 years**

Ho Ho, who lies here?
The good earl of Devonshire
With Maud my Wife
To me full dear
We lived together 50 year.

Here lies
Betty Law
I say no more
She was alive
in twenty five

Here lies
Father and Mother
And sister and I
We all died within
one short year
They all be buried
at Wimble
except I
And I be buried here.

But having gone equipped with paper, pencil and crayon it is difficult to decide what to draw. It is best to select a particular topic (for example, church windows, carvings in wood, church furniture) and concentrate upon this one area in each church you visit. This will enable you to build up a collection of similar things which you can then compare. It will also help you to become a 'specialist' comparatively quickly.*

It is surprising how many variations may be found in the font, for example, surely one of the simplest pieces of church furniture. Some fonts are over 1,000 years old, some were made in your lifetime; some are roughly hewn chunks of stone, some are exquisitely carved; some have wooden covers which hang from the ceiling of the baptistry; some are lead-lined and lead-encased, some are of marble; some have old bowls and new plinths; some are round, some are hexagonal, some are square.

When a drawing or a rubbing is completed remember to make notes on its reverse side so that you have a record of the church in which you made it. Include in the note the name of the church, the village or town in which it is situated and the date (this will enable you to measure improvements in your work!).

A Norman font, with simple cable decoration, St Enedoc in Cornwall

Saxon font in Berwick Salome Church, Oxfordshire (opposite)

*Topics particularly suitable are: tombs (choose a short time span, say fifty years); bosses, gargoyles, corbels, misericords; internal roofing of the nave, spires and towers.

A twelfth-century font made of lead,
Brookland, Kent, showing all twelve
signs of the zodiac and the farming
activity of each month

Norman font on four pillars in New
Shoreham, Sussex

Happisburgh in Norfolk has a fifteenth-century octagonal font carved with the four evangelists, alternating with angels holding musical instruments

It may be, though, that drawing and making pictures in crayon and pen is not your particular interest. You may prefer to make a written record (a sort of diary) of the churches you have visited and the odd things about them that appeal to you. But whether you record in pictures or in words it is always worthwhile to do your own mini-survey. It will teach you to look carefully both inside and outside the building, and, once you have visited a number of different parishes in an area, enable you to make comparisons. My simple chart (page 25) does not require a great deal of effort to complete. Small sketches can be added to the chart it you so wish.

A font with an elaborately carved wooden canopy, Ewelme, Oxfordshire. The canopy, to prevent holy water being stolen by witches, is raised by a pulley system when the font is used

Josiah Wedgwood, the famous eighteenth-century Staffordshire potter, made this font of black basalt for Cardington, Bedfordshire

So far I have only mentioned ways of recording on paper. There are two other ways which we should not forget – the camera and the portable tape recorder. The camera, if used sensitively, will be able to remind us of things that our pen would never be able to recapture – sunlight behind the tower, dark shadows cast by the yew tree over the porch, the smug expression on the face of the wool merchant kneeling beside his wife on a canopied tomb. The tape recorder can be used to support other areas of your study. For example, it's much easier to 'talk' notes than to write them! However, the recorder should really be used to capture sounds which are unique – a peal of bells, a famous clock or a singing weather vane, or the vicar or verger telling of some person, long since dead, who was associated with the area.

And now one question really remains. What to look for? The chapters which follow provide a number of suggestions.

A possible chart you could use to classify the churches you visit

Chart no. _7_
Date of visit _10/5/72_

Church of St _Eban_ at _Spitwick_

EXTERNAL SURVEY

Tower ⎫ _Tower with broach steeple 119 feet high_
Steeple ⎭ _Weathervane – ploughman and horses_
Porch ✓ _has 18C thatch remover – fire fighting – but no thatch now_
Sundial _None_
Gargoyles _Interesting dragons round tower and above porch_
Other interesting features _Old tomb near porch – Captain Spew_
sea captain 1792, man-o-war on his slab!
Materials used for walls/tower _Dressed limestone_
for roof _Slate and tile_
External length (E–W) _130 feet_

Gargoyle over porch

INTERIOR SURVEY

	Architectural style	Roof	Tombs & monuments	Interesting features
Nave	Norman	Wood – not very interesting or old (or clean!)	Brass under tower 1450 John Platt	Wooden pews 15C Norman font (plain)
Chancel	Early English		Sedilia (2 seat) Piscina Jacobean pulpit	Misericords Squint from N. aisle
Transepts	Early English		N. Transept – Stuart tomb to Sir John Pole gentleman in waiting to Charles I	Stone Saxon coffins
Aisles	Early English		Tablets and hatchments to Pole family, N. aisle.	Modern inscription to 9 miners who died in a pit accident 1956. 3 "vicars" died 1349 – plague?
Other chapels	None			

The Font

Church dates from _1162_
Church furniture of interest _Norman font, modern shaft._
Notable people _C. Dickens said to have worshipped here._

Jacobean pulpit

3 Some architectural terms explained

Simple guide books or information sheets are to be found in many churches. They are a useful source of information, drawing attention to things which are especially note-worthy in the building. Since the writers of guide books use architectural terms, the following more common ones are worth remembering:

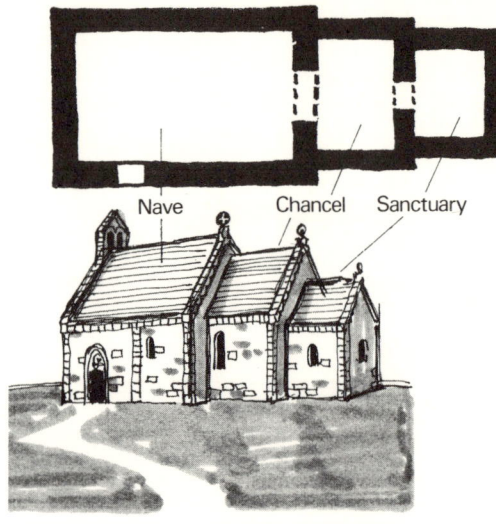

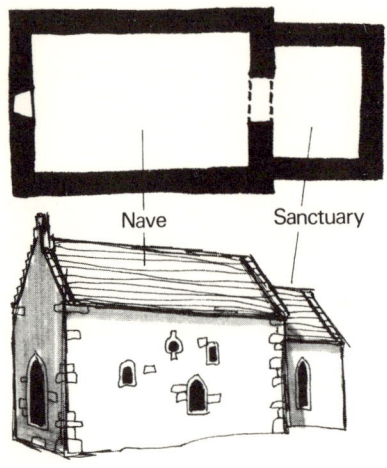

The earliest churches consisted of a **nave** (where the congregation worshipped) and the **sanctuary** which contained the altar. Occasionally the sanctuary was rounded at the east end.

The **chancel** lies between the sanctuary and the nave. Often it contains the choir stalls and is on a slightly higher level than the nave.

Aisles were added by widening the nave. They were useful for processions as well as providing extra accommodation. The north aisle is

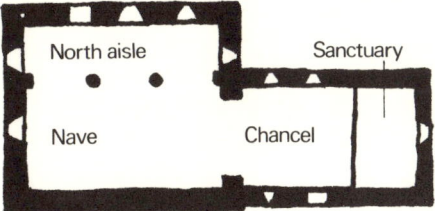

The **porch** is the entrance to the
church. In the plan developed here
the **tower** is usually placed at the
west end. Does your local church
have a tower or spire? At which end
of the building does it stand?
Not all the churches followed this
pattern, but the terms remain the
same.

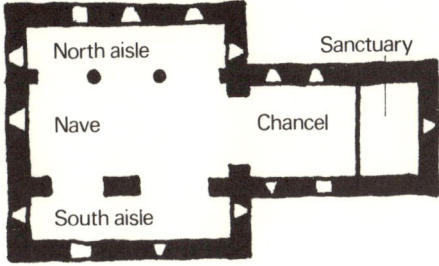

usually older than the south aisle
because the south side of the church
was used for burial.

Does this apply to the churches you
have visited?

*The Holy Sepulchre Church in Cambridge
has a circular Norman nave*

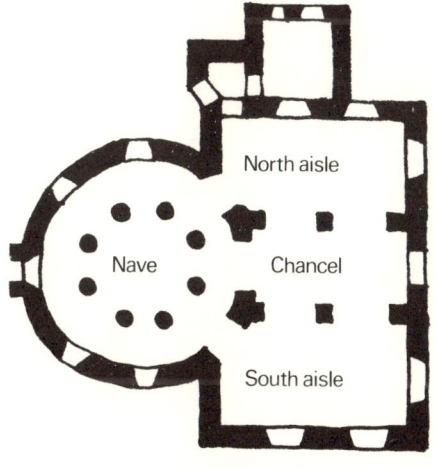

Dent Church, Yorkshire

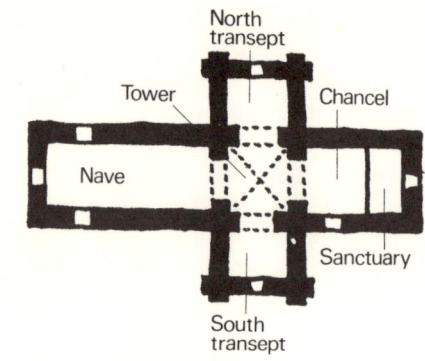

Fairford Church, Gloucestershire

Some churches have their towers between the sanctuary and the nave. On either side of the tower lie the **transepts.** The transepts make the plan of the church look like a cross.

Churches with transepts often have aisles as well. The difference between chancel and sanctuary is sometimes not shown on the plans, the **sanctuary** being the small enclosed space where the **altar** stands within the chancel.

Modern churches sometimes follow the traditional pattern of chancel, aisle and transepts.

However, new materials (concrete and glass) have encouraged architects to experiment with new and exciting shapes.

Is there a modern church near your home?

Could you draw the plan?

Is there a recognisable chancel or nave?

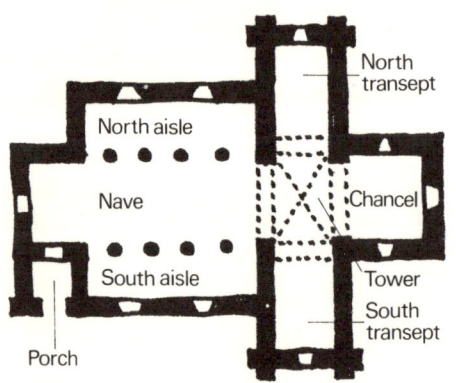

Another way of looking at a church

*The Church of Our Lady of Fatima,
Harlow New Town, Essex, built in 1960*

Tower

Altar

Chancel

Nave

Aisle

Transept

Porch

4 Things to look for outside the church

This chapter – and the one which follows – is really a series of questions. Some answers are suggested which, though generally true, might not relate to every church you visit.

Seventeenth-century lych-gate at Worth in Sussex

1 The churchyard

Is there a lych-gate? Lych is the Saxon word for dead body. The roof over the gate sheltered the body as it was moved from the cart onto the parish bier (a wheeled trolley for

A very worn Saxon cross in the churchyard of Yarnton, Oxfordshire (opposite)

carrying the body from the roadway into the church). It is only in comparatively recent times that coffins have been used for any but the rich.*

Are there any noteworthy tombs, crosses, memorials? Look on the south side of the church. Can you see any evidence of there having been a cross on the site? Before the Reformation the churchyard cross was often

A realistic skull is carved on this early eighteenth-century family tomb

used for preaching and for making proclamations.

Are there any yew trees? These trees were sacred in pagan Britain. It was also a custom in the Mediterranean countries to plant evergreen trees in graveyards, and the custom may have been brought to Britain by priests who had been trained in Rome. Yew tree branches were sold in Tudor times to make bows and arrows.

*In 1678 an Act of Parliament decreed that the dead should be buried in a woollen shroud. This was to help the woollen industry. It was repealed in 1814.

Medieval churchyard cross at Castle Rising, Norfolk. Sometimes there is a hole in the stem where the holy vessels were stored

Four-storied Saxon tower at Bishopstone, Sussex. The corbel-table and cap were added later by the Normans

The evergreen leaves and red berries of a yew tree. The berries are very pretty, but don't forget that they are extremely poisonous

2 The church

Has it a tower? The tower was sometimes a place of refuge in troubled times. Is it in the centre of the church or at the west end, or is it detached from the church altogether? Most towers are square, but occasionally you may find one that is octagonal, round or triangular. Round towers are usually found in areas where good building stone is scarce (like Norfolk). Has the church more than one tower? If it has, can you account for this?

An eleventh-century round tower of flints, Bessingham, Norfolk. Round towers were often built in counties where there were no large rocks to use as cornerstones

Norman tower of Old Shoreham, Sussex

A timber tower – this is the unusual belfry of Brookland Church, Kent, which was built entirely of wood about 1260, and stands detached from the church

THE UPKEEP OF THIS
ANCIENT CHURCH IS A
HEAVY DRAIN
POPULATI

A saddleback tower usually has one gable, but Fingest in Buckinghamshire has two

Transitional tower, New Shoreham, showing the change from round to pointed-arch windows

Octagonal tower, Marsh Baldon, Oxford-shire

Perpendicular towers like Charing, Kent, often have a stair turret

Has it a spire? The spire is really an extension of the tower. All spires are post-Norman (though spires were often added to Norman towers). The purpose of the tower and the spire was to house the bells, though some had the additional role of providing landmarks for sailors.

Parapet spire, Cassington, Oxfordshire

Fourteenth-century broach spire, Detling, Kent. The broach is the triangular block at each corner

Thirteenth-century tower with a lead spire and four pinnacles, Long Sutton, Lincolnshire – lead weathers white, copper turns green (left)

Sir Christopher Wren's 'spire' for St Mary-le-Bow, Cheapside, London, is really a steeple and was built in 1680 (centre)

Louth in Lincolnshire has a parapet spire with flying buttresses; the stone knobs on the spire are called 'crockets' and form steps for steeplejacks (right)

Is there a weather vane? What
does it represent? You will find
weather vanes shaped like violins,
ploughteams, keys, ships, fishes and
even people. The most common
shape, however, is of the cockerel, the
emblem of St Peter. See if you can
find the reason for this (Matthew,
Chapter 26: vv 69–75 and Matthew,
Chapter 16: v 18 contain clues).
Some weather vanes are hollow and
trumpet in the wind.

Is there a public clock? This will
only be worth noting if it has an
unusual face or is of historical signi-
ficance, e.g. a clock showing the
phases of the sun and moon, a clock
which has 'jacks'.

*An old weather vane, now replaced and
given a home inside Church Handborough,
Oxfordshire*

*The mechanism of a very early clock, also
retired and displayed in Church Handborough*

*Gilded clock jacks that still strike the
quarter hour in Rye, Sussex*

What is the main body of the church made of? Many of our churches are built in limestone (a stone found right across Britain from Somerset to North Yorkshire). In some areas, however, granite, red sandstone, flint, brick and even wood predominate. If the church is built of granite or sandstone what do you notice about the stone carvings?

Is there any evidence of a scratch dial in the south wall? The rough circle is usually divided into segments 15 degrees apart, radiating from a shallow hole at the centre. In this hole there might have been a metal gnomon (or rod) which would cast a

Saxon sundial over the door to March Baldon, Oxfordshire, and three scratch dials beside the door of Barfreystone, Kent

shadow across the scratch face, depending, of course, on the height of the sun. More probably the hole was for centring a wooden stick which the passer-by would have to find for himself. If you find a scratch dial, test it in a similar fashion. Could you make an accurate scratch clock on a wall or fence?

Are there any mason's marks?

These were marks lightly cut into the surface of the dressed stone to identify it as the work of a particular mason. Do not confuse these with the special crosses which were carved into the side of the building (twelve in all) for the bishop to bless at the consecration service. These crosses are usually about eight feet above the ground. Sometimes below them you can see a hole. This held a bracket in which a candle was fixed. The bishop, standing on a short ladder, anointed each cross with holy oil.

A consecration cross, Carleton Rode, Norfolk

Are there any gargoyles? These are water spouts taking rain water from the roof. Often they are carved into dragons and demons to frighten away evil spirits from the church and the churchyard.

Masons' marks

Fearsome stone gargoyle from St George's Chapel, Windsor

Two gargoyles on Garsington church, Oxfordshire – perhaps you can invent your own! (opposite)

A mortsafe was a late eighteenth-century means of preventing body snatches —stealing the dead before burial

What is the roof made of? Is it slate, thatched or tiled? Why are thatched roofs more common in some counties than in others?

Hales Church in Norfolk, built of flint, has a thatched roof, a Saxon round tower and an apse

Is there a porch? In mediaeval times the porch became the place from which the parish was administered and often public notices were pinned there. Is this still the case? Are there any other odd things about the porch. Does it, for example, contain fire-fighting equipment, a coracle, or a mortsafe? Is there a room above ground level? (This was often the village armoury.)

**What doorways/entrances are
there to the building?** On what
side of the church do they lie? Are
the door arches highly decorated?
If they are, to what period does the
decoration belong?

*The beautifully decorated early Norman
south doorway to Barfreystone Church,
Kent*

5 Things to look for inside the church

In Chapter 3 I explained the terms used to describe the 'geography' of the church (e.g. nave, aisle, sanctuary, chancel). Here we are not so much concerned with the pattern of the interior shell but of the things found within it. As in the previous chapter the questions can be applied to almost any church in any part of the country.

1 The building

Windows: how are they shaped? Is the style uniform? The windows will help to 'date' the period in which the church was built. They might also suggest periodic rebuilding. Examine the windows both from the inside and from the outside of the building. Do you notice anything? Do they give an idea of the thickness of the walls?

Look for a low side window (usually at the west end of the chancel). These are sometimes called 'leper' windows (through which lepers could watch the service) or confessional windows. In all probability these were used to hold a sanctus bell, which when rung could be heard both inside and outside the building, so that all the

Saxon arch, Escomb, County Durham

villagers would know that a service was in progress (even if some of them were working in the fields). Some experts suggest that they were simply openings in which gifts were left for the priest.

Arches: do they belong to one particular period? Does the style change (e.g. around the tower?). Is there evidence of continual building eastwards or westwards? Is the north aisle older than the south aisle (see page 27). Is there a clearly defined chancel arch?

Saxon

Norman

Transitional

Exterior view

Interior view

A low-side window (Melton Constable, Norfolk)

Early English

Decorated

Perpendicular

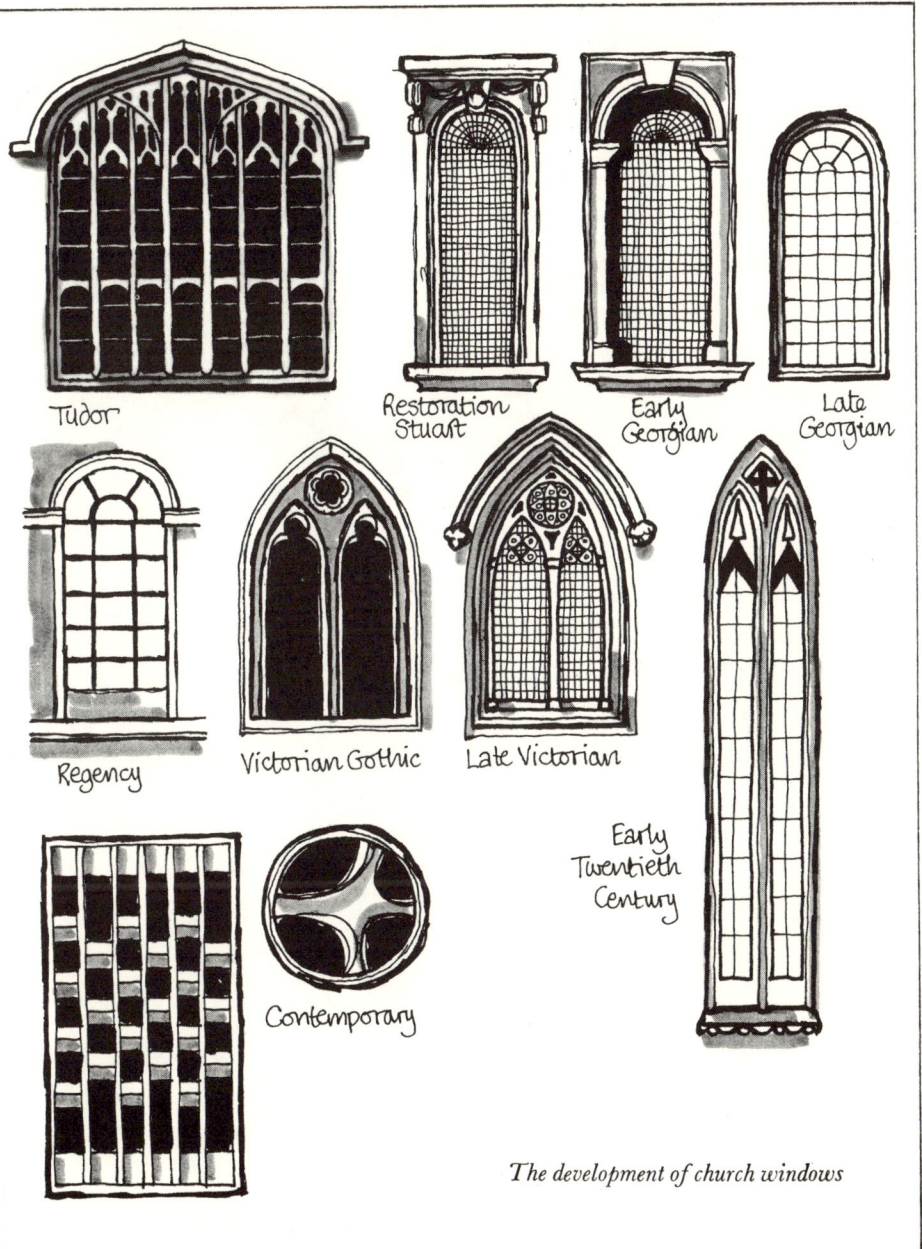

Tudor

Restoration Stuart

Early Georgian

Late Georgian

Regency

Victorian Gothic

Late Victorian

Early Twentieth Century

Contemporary

The development of church windows

Norman arches, Melbourne, Derbyshire

Transitional arches, New Shoreham, Sussex

Early English Arches, Stone, Kent

Is the church lit by windows above the arches of the nave?
Often the nave was extended upwards as well as outwards (i.e. the aisles). This development, often as an addition to buildings which were originally Norman or Transitional, gave a feeling of spaciousness as well as more light. This range of upper windows is known as the clerestory. Many churches (particularly those dating from 1250) were built with a clerestory, but even when this was the case, a slight change in style is often noticeable. Does this hint at the length of time it must have taken to build one of our larger parish churches? Sometimes there is a

Perpendicular arches, Chipping Campden, Gloucestershire

A Norman chancel arch, Old Shoreham, Sussex

Clerestory windows above the south aisle of Cobham, Kent

passage over the aisle beneath the clerestory windows. This is called the triforium.

Is the roof made of stone, wood, or wood and plaster? In what style is it built? Are there any interesting bosses or other forms of roof decoration? Is it gilded or painted?

A fourteenth-century trussed rafter roof in Chartham, Kent

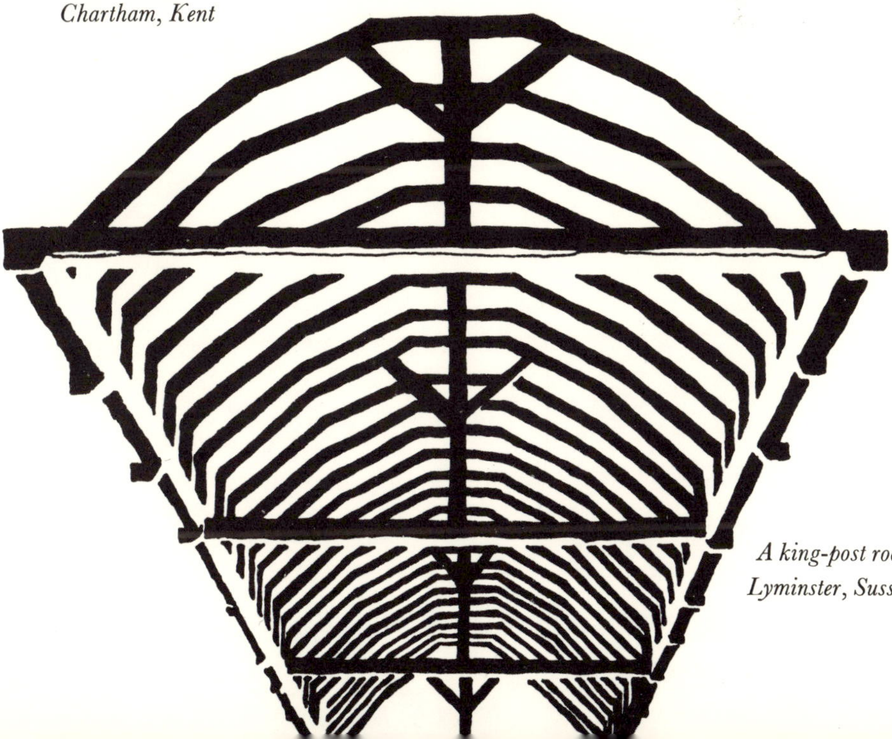

A king-post roof, Lyminster, Sussex

Wagon roof – some are plastered white between the beams, this one is brightly painted

(opposite)
Splendidly carved firred beam roof of St John's Chapel, Ewelme, Oxfordshire

Seventeenth-century hammer beam roof,
Plaxtol, Kent. This church is not
dedicated to any saint because it was
built during the Reformation

(opposite)
This tie beam roof in Charing Church,
Kent, is painted to look like carving. It is
dated 1592 and also inscribed 'ER 34' –
what does this mean?
To discover the derivation of the word
'nave', turn this illustration upside-down.
Of what does it remind you?

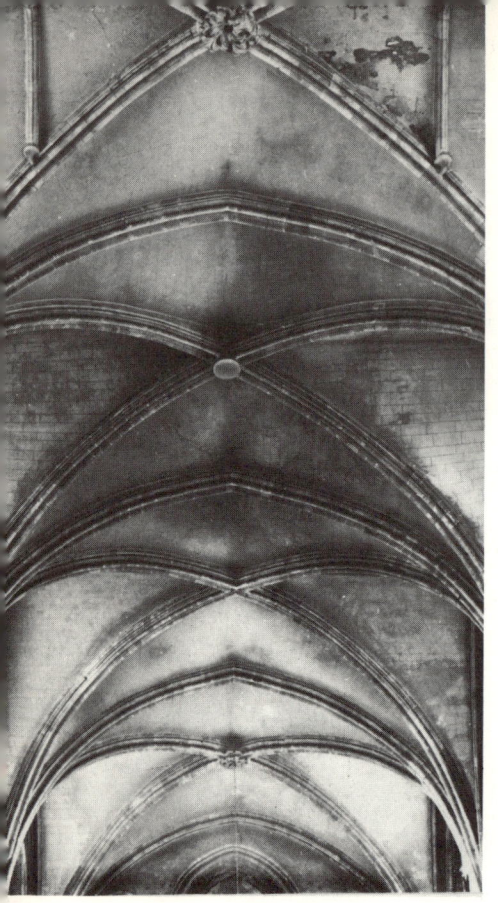

Lierne vaulting from Tewkesbury choir,
Gloucestershire (fourteenth century)

Quadripartite stone-vaulted roof at New
Shoreham, Sussex (thirteenth century)

Tierceron vaulting (fourteenth century)

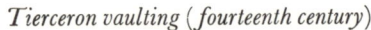

(opposite)
Fan vaulting in North Leigh, Oxfordshire
(fifteenth century)

A carved roof boss from the south porch of Stoke-by-Nayland Church, Suffolk

What is the characteristic decoration around windows and arches? This is another reliable method of dating a building, particularly if the motifs are studied together with the shape of windows, doorways, columns and arches and with roof styles.

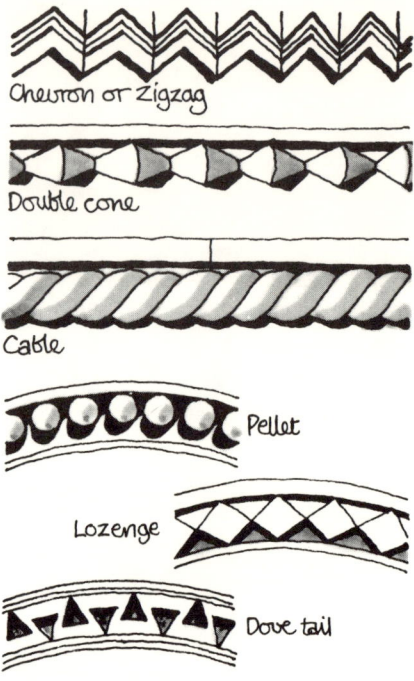

Chevron or Zigzag

Double cone

Cable

Pellet

Lozenge

Dove tail

Norman decoration

Dog tooth

Three-leaf flower

Early English

Billet

Nail head

Beak head

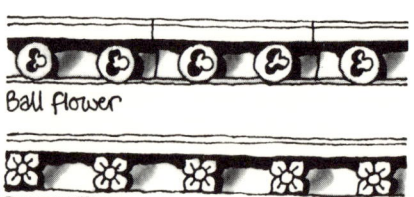

Ball flower

Tablet flower

Decorated

Perpendicular

Brattishing

Tudor rose

Tudor

*The alabaster tomb of Ralph and
Katheren Green in Lowick,
Northamptonshire . . .*

2 Monuments and tombs

Which is the oldest tomb in the church? Is the grave marked by a simple slab? If there is an ornate effigy, is it topped by an ornate canopy? Is it made of stone or of wood? Effigies on tombs were usually made to show the person commemorated in healthy early middle age, for it was thought that this is how the person would appear at the final resurrection. Sometimes the tombs were made like bunk beds – the person is shown twice, once in the best of health and once as a corpse.* Try to make a series of sketches or notes of the different tombs that you can see. With experience you will be able to make fairly accurate guesses as to the date of burial. For example, knights dressed in chain mail date from before 1300, civilians with forked beards between 1295–1360,

*A cadaver.

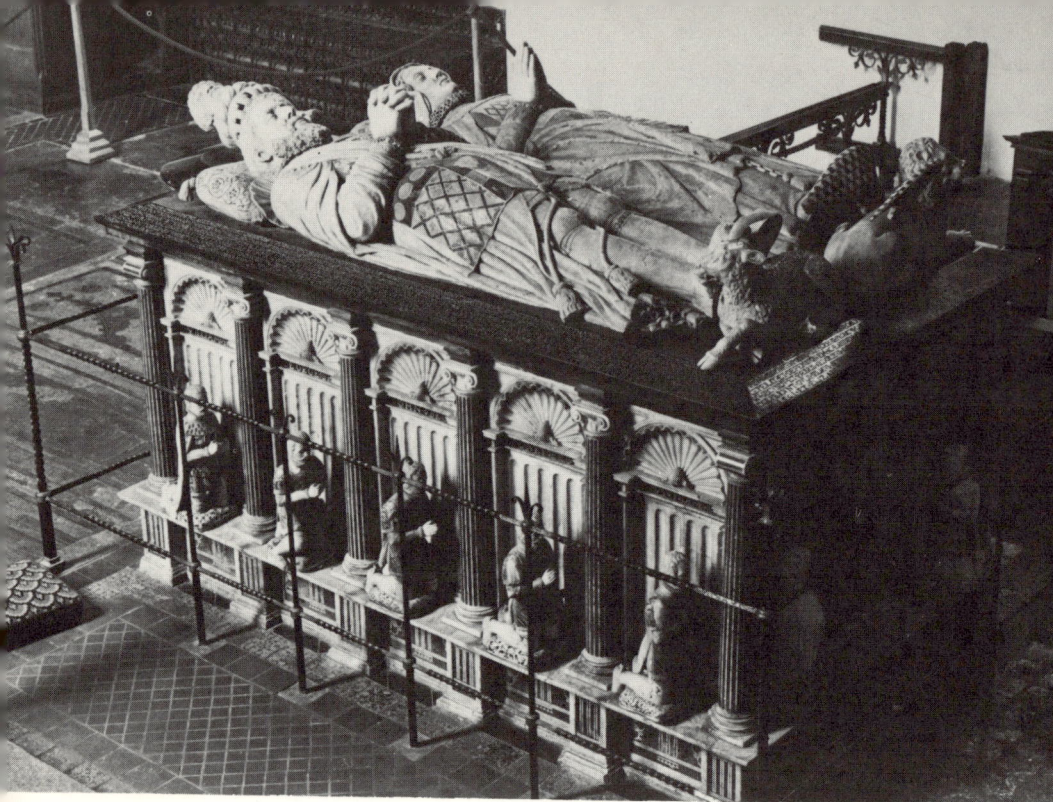

. . . and Lord Cobham and his wife Ann Bray in Cobham Church, Kent Which tomb is the earlier?

ladies with veils and wimples (head coverings) between 1270–1320. Do any of the tombs or memorials commemorate famous people? Do the tombs give us any indication of the age of the building?

Are there any hatchments hanging in the church? Do these relate to any of the tombs or plaques? Hatchments date from about 1600. They are large paintings on wood, framed in black, of the shield, crest and motto of the dead person. They were at first hung in the front of the dead person's house for the period of mourning, before being brought into the church.

3 Stone fittings

Look for the following:
A water stoup (basin), usually situated near the porch. It once contained holy water.

The font. See pages 20–24.

A stone or wooden rood screen. This will be found below the chancel arch, separating the nave (the people's part of the church) from the choir/chancel/sanctuary in which the priest performs his rites. Many were pulled down at the Reformation.

Rood screens were made of stone, or wood, like this fifteenth-century screen in Scarning Church, Norfolk

A squint, which is an opening in an inside wall to give a view of the high altar so that Masses could be said simultaneously in different parts of the church. The opening is often angled. The squint is sometimes called a hagioscope.

Interior **consecration crosses,** usually painted (see page 43).

A piscina, a shallow basin, near an altar, for washing sacred vessels after Mass. These are usually found on the south wall. If there is a piscina but no altar what does this tell us? Occasionally piscinas are double (i.e. two side by side). Experts suggest these were installed only between 1270–1310.

Early fourteenth-century double piscina,
Cobham, Kent

Sedilia. Seats usually in the south
wall of the chancel near the altar.
Has the sedilia two, three or four
seats?

A triple sedilia coupled under elaborate canopies with a piscina; also in Cobham Church

A corbel. This is a stone which projects from the wall to carry weight, e.g. roof timbers, stone vaulting. Often the corbels are fantastically carved. 'Corbel' is used to describe stone supports both inside and outside the building. A line of corbels (e.g. along the top of the external nave wall) is called a corbel table.

An aumbry. A small safe (often now little more than a hole in the stone wall) in which the sacred vessels were locked.

A reredos. A carved screen behind the altar. Carved stone screens are still to be found in many of the larger churches. Few figures in the stone niches will be as old as the screen. At the Reformation carved images were destroyed, particularly during the Commonwealth (1649–1660).

Carved stone corbel in Ewelme Church, Oxfordshire

A cresset stone. A stone in which holes had been cut. The holes were filled with oil and lighted wicks were floated in the oil . . . in effect a primitive form of candle lighting.

A plaster reredos, dated about 1400, in the north transept of Thaxted, Essex. The sculpted figures were removed from the niches of most reredos in the Reformation

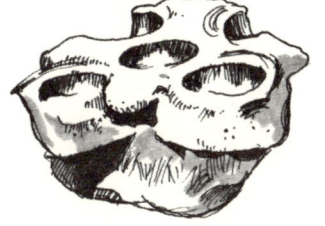

4 Church furniture

Look for the following:

Carved stalls (usually in the chancel). Look particularly for carving beneath any seats which fold upwards. These *misericords* often provide interesting comment on life in mediæval Britain.

Bench ends on pews, which may be of two types, rectangular or shaped.*

Cresset stones—these are rare. The lower stone, for example, is the only one in Essex, at Blackmore Church

Fourteenth-century misericord from Etchingham, Kent, showing Reynard the Fox dressed as a bishop, preaching to geese

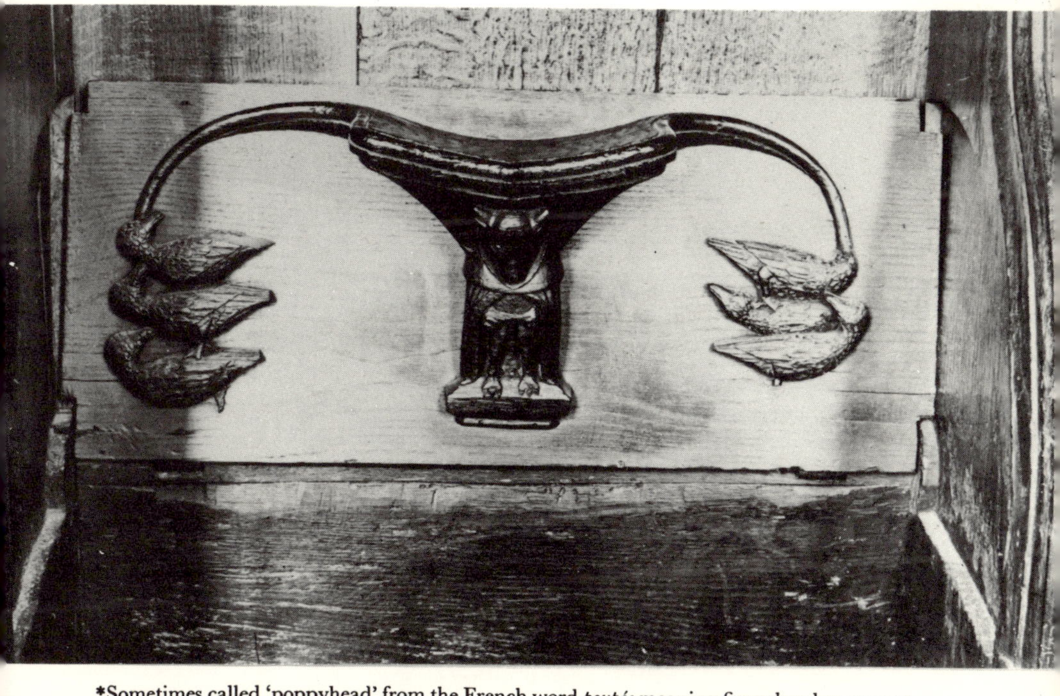

*Sometimes called 'poppyhead' from the French word *poupée* meaning figurehead or puppet.

Does the church contain any carved bench ends? Do they tell us anything about the life and times of the men who carved them?

Box pews usually date from Georgian times. If the church has box pews do they contain anything odd – a fireplace, for example? (These were sometimes used for baking communion bread.)

Kneelers. Are there any embroidered kneelers which give an indication of the history of the area?

Simple 'poppyhead' bench end, Old Shoreham, Sussex

Carved bench end with a fine 'poppyhead' and image of Jack-in-the-Green, the Spirit of Nature, in Charing, Kent

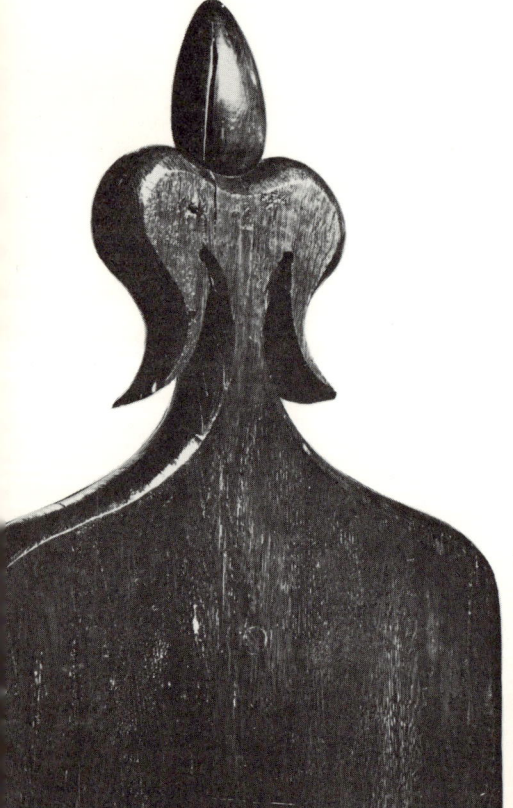

A typical West Country square-headed bench end in Braunton Church, Devon, carved with a lantern and thirty pieces of silver; from a series depicting the Passion

Chests. Has the church an old chest? Chests were used to keep registers, precious vestments and plate. Often they have more than one lock, so that several people would need to be present each time it was opened (one person, one key). Has the chest a hole in the lid for collections?

Wimborne Minster in Dorset possesses this 6½ feet long Saxon dugout chest; the actual cavity is only 22 × 9 × 6 inches

Fourteenth-century heavily iron-bound chest, Copford, Essex

The Jacobean wood pulpit in Beckley Church, Oxfordshire, has a sounding board, a candlestick and, on the wall to the right, an hour glass in a holder

Fourteenth-century wooden lectern, Detling, Kent

Medieval wooden eagle lectern in
Monksilver, Somerset

The pulpit. Is it made of wood or stone? Has it a sounding board? Has it an hour glass (so that the preacher could time the length of his sermons)? Pulpits became an essential part of church furniture in 1547. Can you suggest why they were not common before this?

The lectern, the stand from which the Bible is read. Is the lectern made of wood or metal?* Is it a plain stand (like a reading desk) or is it made in the form of an animal or bird? The eagle is the shape most usually found – representing the gospel flying around the world. How is the lectern supported? Are there any interesting designs or carvings round the base?

Is there a chained Bible?

Of course this list is not all-embracing. Every old church will have something which is unique, something peculiarly its own. In one you might find an interesting collection of books, in another musical instruments, in a third an exhibition of state seals.

It is this which makes the church such a worthwhile place to visit.

*Very rarely lecterns were made of stone.

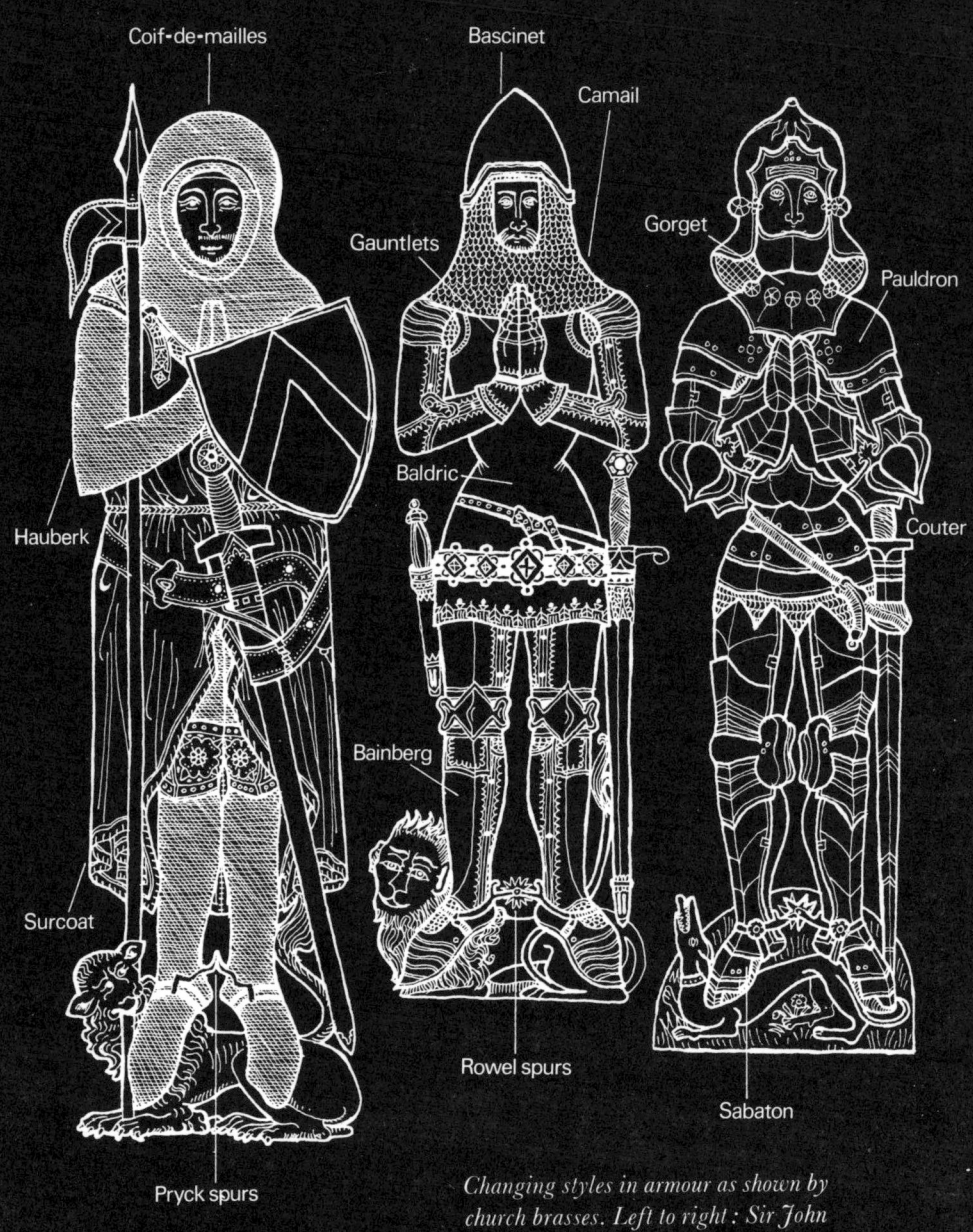

Coif-de-mailles

Bascinet

Camail

Gauntlets

Gorget

Pauldron

Hauberk

Baldric

Couter

Surcoat

Bainberg

Rowel spurs

Sabaton

Pryck spurs

Changing styles in armour as shown by church brasses. Left to right : Sir John D'Abernoun, Sheriff of Surrey, 1277, the oldest brass in England (Stoke D'Abernon Church, Surrey) ; a member of the Dalison family, about 1400 (Laughton, Lincolnshire) ; Edmond Clere, 1488 (Stokesby, Norfolk)

6 What's in a name?

When a church is consecrated (that is made a church by the bishop) it is also dedicated. This means that it is named in memory of a person (or a group of persons), an event, or sometimes even of a place. Occasionally the church's dedication commemorates some aspect of Christian faith. Thus to give examples of each of the above, the church might be dedicated to Alfred, St Peter and St Paul, The English Martyrs, The Holy Sepulchre, The Holy Trinity. Most of the saints have an 'emblem' associated with them; these often appear in the church in the most unlikely places, e.g. around a corbel, a carving in a roof, on a bench end, on a misericord, in a stained-glass window, or on an embroidered kneeler. The emblem often incorporates some aspect of the saint's life and the manner of his death. For example, James the Great has a scallop shell. The scallop shell was used in mediaeval times as a 'pilgrim mark' (that the person possessing a brooch made in the form of this shell had been or was on a pilgrimage). St James was the first missionary – one who travelled for Christ. Bartholomew's emblem is a butcher's knife; it was with a 'flaying knife' that he was executed.

Briefly we can classify church dedications under the following headings:

1 Biblical

These would include all those associated with Christ during his lifetime and the period following immediately upon it.

Saint	Emblem
Mary, mother of Jesus	a lily
The Evangelists – the writers of gospels	
John	an eagle
Luke	an ox
Mark	a lion
Matthew	a winged man
Andrew	a diagonal cross
Bartholomew	a butcher's flaying knife
James the Great	a scallop shell
James the Less	a club
John the Baptist	a lamb or a lamb on a book
Joseph of Arimathea	flowering staff
Jude	a boat or a club
Mary Magdalene	ointment pot
Matthias	axe or sword
Peter	keys
Philip	loaves and fishes

Simon	a saw or fish
Stephen	stones and a book
Thomas	a book and/or a spear

2 Historical figures

The dedication of a church to an historical figure very often gives a clue to the person who founded the first church on the site. For example, there are a number of churches in Dorset dedicated to Adhelm, who was a missionary in the West Country during the seventh century. No churches are dedicated to him elsewhere. Similarly churches dedicated to Felix (d 648) are all found on the east coast. It was Felix who brought Christianity to the East Angles.

Another reason for dedication to a particular saint might be that the original founder (e.g. a powerful lord or a local abbot) regarded the saint as being his 'personal' saint (the one to whom he prayed for help when in difficulties or distress) or the saint of his particular religious order:

A modern statue of St Aiden on Holy Island, Northumberland

Aiden	d 651	Missionary to Northumbria.
Alban	d 304	First English Martyr.
Aldhelm	d 709	Missionary to Dorset, Devon, Cornwall.
Alfred	d 899	King of Wessex.
Alphage	d 1012	Executed at Greenwich, London, by Danes.
Anselm	d 1109	Archbishop of Canterbury.
Antony	d 356	Egyptian saint. His emblem is a pig and a bell.
Audrey		See Etheldreda.
Augustine	d 604	Missionary to the Saxons (see page 11), first Archbishop of Canterbury.
Bede	d 735	'The Monk of Jarrow'. Bede wrote a *History of the English Church and People*.
Birinus	d c 650	Missionary to Wessex.
Blaise	d 303	Bishop in Asia Minor; patron saint of wool combers and of sufferers with throat ailments, also doctors and dentists.
Boniface	d 754	English missionary to Germany.
Botolph	d 655	Founded an Abbey in Lincolnshire at Boston. Often shown holding a church in his hand.
Catherine	d c 350	An early Christian martyr—remembered for her martyrdom on a wheel. Patron saint of students, millers, wagon builders and teachers. Her emblem is a spiked wheel.
Chad	d 672	Missionary to Mercia (Derbyshire, Staffordshire). He is often remembered in association with his equally famous brother Cedd.
Charles	d 1649	Charles I, the Stuart king who was executed by Cromwell.
Columba	d 597	Irish missionary. He founded the famous monastery on the Island of Iona.

Crispin	d 287	Patron saint of shoemakers.
Cuthbert	d 687	Scottish missionary, who is usually associated with the Holy Island of Lindisfarne.
David	d 603	Welsh missionary. Patron saint of Wales.
Dunstan	d 988	Archbishop of Canterbury. He was artistic and enjoyed working with his hands. He is the patron saint of goldsmiths and his emblem is a pair of pincers.
Edmund	d 866	King of East Anglia. He was martyred by the Danes and is often shown carrying arrows. Bury St Edmunds is named after him.
Edward the Confessor	d 1066	The founder of Westminster Abbey.
Ethelbert	d 616	King of Kent, converted by Augustine.
Etheldreda	d 679	The founder of the monastery at Ely.
Felix	d 648	Missionary to East Anglia.
Giles	d c 750	A Greek missionary to France. Patron saint of sick children and cripples. His emblem is a deer and an arrow.
Hilda	d 680	A famous abbess of the equally famous monastery at Whitby.
Hugh	d 1200	Bishop of Lincoln, famous for his pet swan which became his emblem.
Laurence	d 258	Roman deacon, martyred on a gridiron which became his emblem.
Leonard	d 559	A French saint, remembered for freeing slaves. His emblem is a chain or fetter.
Martin	d 397	Bishop of Tours (France).
Melitus	d 624	First Bishop of London.
Nicholas	d 350	The saint of children (Santa Claus) and sailors. He is also the patron saint of pawnbrokers and his emblem is three golden balls.
Oswald	d 642	King of Northumbria. His emblem is a sceptre and a cross.

Osyth	d c 653	Queen of the East Saxons and founder of an Essex nunnery.
Pancras	d 304	A Roman boy martyr. His emblems are a sword and a stone.
Patrick	d 461	Patron saint of Ireland.
Paulinus	d 644	First Bishop of York.
Richard of Chichester	d 1253	A famous Bishop of Chichester. Often shown with a silver or golden goblet.
Swithin	d 862	Bishop of Winchester; he is associated with the legend that should it rain on July 15th it will continue wet for the forty days which follow.
Thomas (à Becket)	d 1170	The martyr of Canterbury who was killed by Henry II's knights. His shrine became the principal place of pilgrimage in mediaeval England.
Thomas More	d 1535	Lord Chancellor of England, executed by Henry VIII.
Wilfred	d 709	A famous Bishop of York.

3 Legendary figures

The term 'legendary' is a little misleading. Although people like Helen and George certainly lived, so many stories were embroidered around their lives after their deaths that it is difficult to disentangle fact from fiction.

Archangels Michael	
Gabriel	
Raphael	
Christopher	Patron saint of travellers.
George	Patron saint of England. His emblem is a red cross on a white ground. He is often shown fighting the legendary dragon.
Helen	Helen lived in the fourth century. It has been said that her father was the original 'Old King Cole' of Colchester.

ST MARTIN-IN-THE-FIELDS

St Martin giving his cloak to a beggar is the subject of this panel, St Martin-in-the-Fields, London

Uncumber	A lady saint who grew a beard to prevent her ever being married.
Veronica	Veronica is shown holding a towel with which she wiped the face of Christ on the road to Calvary.

The study of saints has a very impressive name – hagiology. The lists above are meant only as a starting point for further research. How many different saints can you find recorded in a single church, in a city (where there are a number of churches), or in your county? How often do the same saints re-occur? You could also try to link saints with occupations. For example, Tibba is the patron saint of falconers, St Hunna, the patron saint of washer-women, while St Zita looks after the interests (heavenly and earthly) of serving maids. What unusual occupational links can you find?

Margaret (of Antioch)	Guardian of women in child-birth. The devil, disguised as a dragon, visited her as she lay in prison. She forced the devil to help her escape.

Another way of collecting information is by making drawings of the symbols of saints that you see in the churches you visit.

7 Curiosities

It is because all churches are different that they are worth studying. Whenever I go into an old building I look for the things which make it quite different from any other that I have ever visited . . . and, of course, it is the odd, curious things that I tend to remember.

This chapter, then, is really little more than a collection of jottings. If you choose to make a collection of curiosities, the following headings indicate the direction your study might take:

Things out of place
A fire engine, a scold's bridle (for a nagging wife), stocks and pillories, an open fire-place to warm a family pew, a knight's helm and a sword, a rifle, a boat, church bells at ground level in a wooden house of their own.

Things written
A library of rare books (usually found above the porch or in the tower room), a chained Bible, old manuscripts and registers.

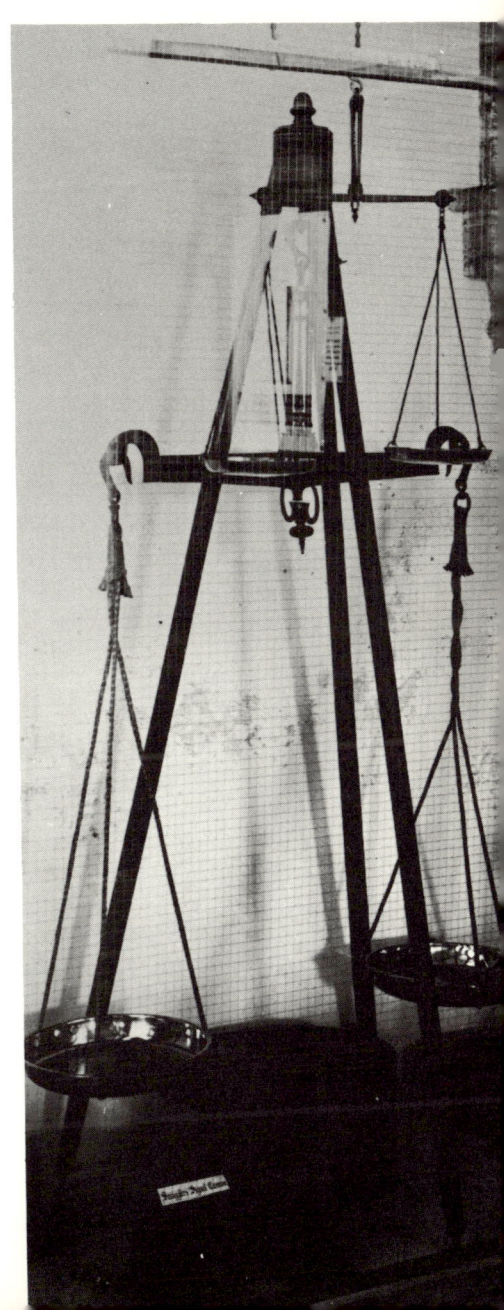

Perhaps out of place inside a church – 1795 tithe scales in Brookland, Kent. The church also displays a smuggler's signal cannon

Things strange
A disused school room (now a chapel), holes made by Roundhead bullets, effigies without noses (removed by Puritan swords) a memorial to a pet.

Things painted
Ceilings and walls, chests and tombs, pictures of the church in previous centuries.

Things buried
Unconventional tombs – like that of the man who wanted to be buried half in the church and half out of it, half above the ground and half below it (and was) . . . or the knight holding his lady's hand.

Things recorded
On tombs, on chests, on the church walls. Information about battles, events (a local disaster), people (like the doctor whose pills could cure everything from gout to blindness), and families (like the Mayor of Abingdon whose memorial lists his descendants).

Things royal
A royal burial, a royal wedding, a royal name (like Bere Regis) . . . or is the church itself a royal peculiar?

Things seen in glass
Stories of saints, kings, poets, explorers, artists and even life in times past.

Things in metal
A chalice worked by a mediaeval

St Dunstan's in the West, an eighteenth-century church in Fleet Street, London, unexpectedly has a 1586 statue of Elizabeth I

QUEEN ELIZABETH

1530 merchant ship in glass

silversmith, a pewter plate, a cross from Ethiopia, a sculpture by Epstein or Rodin.

Things in wood
The carvings and mouldings of master workmen, and their 'signatures' (like the split pea on the work of Grinling Gibbons).

Things musical
From hand-powered organs to harmoniums, trumpets and bells.

Musical instruments in stone: bagpipes, twin pipes and kettle drums – known in medieval times as 'nakers' . . .

. . . and in glass, a fifteenth-century angel playing a rebeck

Things architectural
Was the church built by a famous architect, e.g. Sir Christopher Wren (1632–1723), Nicolas Hawksmoor (1661–1736), Augustus Pugin (1812–1852) or Basil Spence (b 1907)?

Things confusing
A church with two naves, or five aisles, a church which has two towers and a spire; a church with a leaning tower or a crooked spire.

Things mathematical
Roman numerals are most often used on monuments.

Remember that:

1	I	20	XX
2	II	40	XL
3	III	50	L
4	IV	60	LX
5	V	90	XC
6	VI	100	C
7	VII	300	CCC
8	VIII	400	CD
9	IX	500	D
10	X	600	DC
		1000	M

Things Latin
Many old tombs have Latin inscriptions. The following might help you glean a little from the inscription:

Hic jacet	here lies
Aetatis suae, aet	in his or her age
Obiit, Ob:	died

*Something confusing – Barfreystone in
Kent has no belfry, so the bell is hung
in a yew tree*

Hic jacet Charles Worth ob:
MDCCV aet LXI
Here lies Charles Worth who died in
1705 aged 61.

8 Some things to do

In Chapter 2 I described the ways in which you could make a record of the churches you visit by sketching and by taking rubbings. Having built up a collection of drawings, notes and scraps of interesting information, there remains the task of classifying your findings in some way. The following suggestions are meant only as a guide, but they do indicate the sort of approach you could attempt.

Scrapbook or loose-leaf folder? Loose-leaf folders are the most satisfactory methods of keeping material. You can continually add information on new sheets to expand a section and re-write sheets should you make mistakes. Loose-leaf folders can be made to any shape and size (a scrapbook tends to become somewhat unwieldy if it becomes too thick). Another advantage of the folder is that you can change the paper according to the topic you are considering. For example, red paper for tombs, green for fonts, black for postcards and photographs. On the other hand, scrapbooks are ideal if you are keeping a diary-type record (for example, when on a holiday or on a school field trip).

Whatever method you choose, mount your selected material with care. This means that adequate space should be left around each piece so that every page has a 'pattern' of its own. It is also worth remembering that only a small amount of paste is necessary to hold each piece in position. A light smear of a reliable adhesive along the top edge will be quite adequate. If you think that you might want to rearrange a page later on, use Cow Gum or rubber paste. These adhesives allow papers to be peeled apart, undamaged, even after a considerable passage of time.

Lettering will also need to done with care. Felt pens are excellent for this, particularly as they enable you to use colour. It is wise – unless your lettering is of high quality – to do your titles on paper and mount them into your book when they are dry. It is easy to throw away a scruffy title and start again, but expensive to tear out page after page of mounting paper. Lettering sets (stencils) offer another possible way of ensuring a high standard as does Letraset (a simple-to-use transfer).

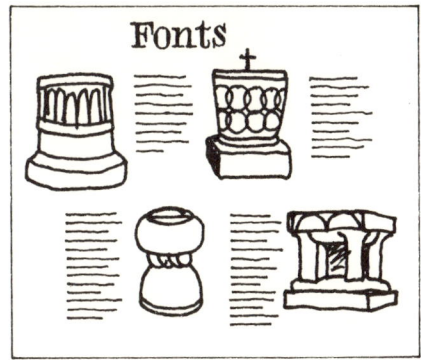

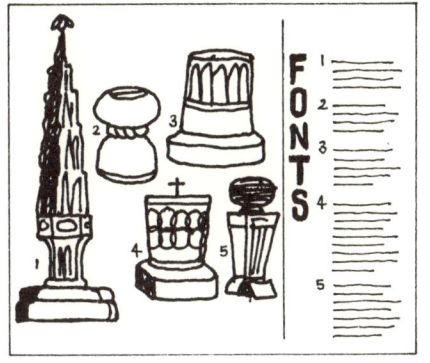

Which of these layouts do you prefer?

Making a book is one way of recording things you have learned. You could also make a model to show the main features of a church. The simplest method is to use boxes which are glued together to give the desired shape. Roofs are made from card. The finished model is covered with paste and paper strips and painted. Windows and fine details are made with coloured paper and glued onto the model when the paint has dried. How will you display your model? If you decide to set it within a churchyard, trees and bushes may be made from wire and cotton wool or from wire wool. Felt makes an excellent 'grass' base. Tombstones made from clay, brick or wood scraps are added last of all.

You will have noticed that many churches have beautiful stained-glass windows. Another art activity you might like to attempt is to design your own.

You will need some cartridge paper

on which to work your design. Draw
it in pencil first and when you are
satisfied with the design, go over your
lines in Indian ink and leave it to dry.
The design lines represent the leads
in the window (see page 81). The
next stage is to add colour. This is
done by filling the areas *between* the
design lines with wax crayon,
heavily and evenly applied. When
the whole window has been worked,
turn the paper over, placing it face
down on a sheet of newspaper.

The window is now made transparent. Take a small twist of cotton
wool and soak it in cooking oil. Apply
the oiled pad to the paper, working
the oil into the surface so that the
paper becomes transparent. When
the oil has dried, crayon can be
applied to the reverse (oiled) side of
the design to heighten or strengthen
colours that appear weak when held
to the sunlight. Display your design
against a window for maximum
effect.

9 A summary of architectural terms

Aisle — Part of the church on either side of a nave or chancel.

Aumbry — Small wall cupboard

Apse — Semi-circular end of chancel.

Boss — A decoration at the junction of the ribs in roof vaulting.

Buttress — An internal or external support for the walls.

Capital — The top part of a column.

Chancel — Eastern part of church.

Chantry — A special chapel set aside for prayers for the dead.

Clerestory — The side wall of the nave above the aisle roof, usually pierced by windows.

Corbel — A stone jutting from a wall to carry weight.

Crossing — The space where the east-west axis of the church is crossed.

Dormer — Window through a roof.

Gargoyle — Stone waterspout.

Lights — The divisions of a window.

Misericords — Hinged wooden seats usually found in the choir.

Parclose — A screen enclosing a chapel.

Piscina — A small hand basin with a drain beside an altar.

Reredos — Ornamental screen at the back of an altar.

Sanctuary — The part of the chancel which contains the altar.

Sedilia — Seats for clergy carved in the south wall of the chancel.

Shaft — A small thin column of stone.

Solar — An upper floor.

Squints — Holes pierced through the chancel arch to give sight of the high altar.

Transept — The transverse part of a cruciform church set at right angles to the east-west axis.

Tympanum — The filling of the arch of a Norman doorway.

Vault — Stone ceiling.

Water stoup — A basin near the porch for holding holy water.

Saxon apse, Worth, Sussex

Fourteenth-century carved timber boss,
Chartham, Kent

Two sturdy pinnacled flying buttresses,
New Shoreham, Sussex

*Buttresses supporting the transept and
tower of Minster Lovell, Oxfordshire*

Curiously sculpted Norman capitals, Old Shoreham, Sussex

Tudor dormer windows, Greensted-Juxta-Ongar, Essex. The church also has a Saxon nave built of split oak trunks, a rare survivor

Norman tympanum carved with a lion
gripping a shield, St Peter with his keys,
and a holy lamb ; Church Handborough,
Oxfordshire

Appendix 1
Dating the building

Often guide books refer to a particular building style, but omit to give the date. This chart might help you.

Ruler	Came to The Throne	Building Style		
William I	1066	Norman		
William II	1087			
Henry I	1100			
Stephen/Matilda	1135			
Henry II	1154			
Richard I	1189			
John	1199		Early English	'Gothic'
Henry III	1216			
Edward I	1272		leading onto	
Edward II	1307			
Edward III	1327		Decorated	
Richard II	1377		Perpendicular	
Henry IV	1399			
Henry V	1413			
Henry VI	1422			
Edward IV	1461			
Edward V	1483			
Richard III	1483			
Henry VII	1485			
Henry VIII	1509			
Edward VI	1547		Renaissance	
Mary	1553			
Elizabeth I	1558			
James I	1603			
Charles I	1625			
Commonwealth (Oliver Cromwell Richard Cromwell!)	1649			
Charles II	1660			

Ruler	Came to The Throne	Building Style
James II	1685	
William & Mary	1689	
Anne	1702	Georgian
George I	1714	
George II	1727	
George III	1760	
George IV	1820	
William IV	1830	
Victoria	1837	Gothic revival
Edward VII	1901	
George V	1910	
Edward VIII	1936	Contemporary
George VI	1936	
Elizabeth II	1952	

Appendix 2 Suppliers of materials

Most of the materials listed in the book are obtainable from your local stationers or your local hardware stores. However, the following list will help you if you experience difficulty.

Art & craft material
Papers & paints (including detail paper & pastel paper)

E. J. Arnold & Co	Butterfly Street, Leeds.
Dryad Ltd	Northgates, Leicester.
Berol Ltd	Ashley Road, Tottenham, London, N.17.
Reeves & Sons Ltd	Lincoln Road, Enfield, Middx.
Rowney & Co, Ltd	Percy Street, London W.1.
Winsor & Newton Ltd	Wealdstone, Harrow, Middx.

Adhesives

Cow Gum	local hardware stores.
Bateman's rubber paste	local stationers.

Dyes & stains

Cold water dyes 'Dylon'	Woolworths and hardware stores.
Ebony Stain	Dryad Ltd, Northgates, Leicester.

Wax crayons

Finart/Freart range of Crayola Crayons	Binney & Smith Ltd, Ampthill Road, Bedford.